# THIRD EDITION

## Let's Begin

## LET'S GO

### STUDENT BOOK

Ritsuko Nakata

Karen Frazier

Barbara Hoskins

with songs and chants by Carolyn Graham

**OXFORD**

UNIVERSITY PRESS

# OXFORD
## UNIVERSITY PRESS

198 Madison Avenue
New York, NY 10016 USA

Great Clarendon Street, Oxford ox2 6dp UK

Oxford University Press is a department of the University of Oxford.
It furthers the University's objective of excellence in research, scholarship,
and education by publishing worldwide in

Oxford  New York

Auckland  Cape Town  Dar es Salaam  Hong Kong  Karachi
Kuala Lumpur  Madrid  Melbourne  Mexico City  Nairobi
New Delhi  Shanghai  Taipei  Toronto

With offices in

Argentina  Austria  Brazil  Chile  Czech Republic  France  Greece
Guatemala  Hungary  Italy  Japan  Poland  Portugal  Singapore
South Korea  Switzerland  Thailand  Turkey  Ukraine  Vietnam

OXFORD and OXFORD ENGLISH are registered trademarks of
Oxford University Press

Senior Editor: Paul Phillips
Associate Editor: Eudie Pak
Art Director: Maj-Britt Hagsted
Design Project Manager: Amelia L. Carling
Designer: Jaclyn Smith, Alicia Dorn (cover)
Art Editor: Elizabeth Blomster
Production Manager: Shanta Persaud
Production Controller: Eve Wong

Student Book:
ISBN-13: 978 0 19 439424 6
ISBN-10: 0 19 439424 7

Student Book with CD-ROM:
ISBN-13: 978 0 19 439431 4
ISBN-10: 0 19 439431 x

Student Book as pack component:
ISBN-13: 978 0 19 439438 3
ISBN-10: 0 19 439438 7

CD-ROM as pack component:
ISBN-13: 978 0 19 439416 1
ISBN-10: 0 19 439416 6

Printed in Hong Kong.

10 9 8 7 6 5 4 3 2 1

ACKNOWLEDGMENTS

Illustrators: COVER: Zina Saunders, Janet Skiles; INTERIOR: Zina Saunders: 2, 3,10,
11, 20, 21, 28, 29, 38, 39, 46, 47, 56, 57,64, 65; Bob Berry: 2, 4, 6, 12, 13, 14, 22, 24,
30, 32, 40, 42, 48, 50, 51, 58, 60, 66, 68; Teresa Anderko: 17, 60, 72; Nan Brooks: 31,
72; Mircea Catusanu: 6, 14, 34, 40, 50, 59, 70; Elizabeth DiGregorio: 5, 48; Patrick
Girouard: 7, 35, 59, 63, 69; Sharon Harmer: 12, 16, 26, 33, 43, 52; Steve Henry: 7,
18, 30, 42, 49, 52, 54, 73; Anthony Lewis: 23, 26, 36, 55, 70; Mindy Pierce: 5, 17,
27, 37, 41, 49, 67, 71; Chris Reed: 16, 19, 25, 35, 44, 53, 54, 58, 60, 72; Deborah
Melmon: 9, 13, 27, 45, 54, 67; Christine Schneider: 4, 15, 41, 52, 73; Dale Simpson:
15, 18, 25, 34, 36, 54, 61; Janet Skiles: 18, 19, 36, 37, 54, 55, 72, 73; Jim Talbot: 3, 4,
6, 9, 10, 11, 12, 13, 14, 16, 17, 20, 21, 22, 24, 26, 27, 28, 29, 30, 32, 34, 35, 38, 39, 40,
42, 43, 44, 45, 46, 47, 48, 50, 52, 53, 56, 57, 58, 60, 62, 63, 64, 65, 66, 67, 68, 69, 70,
71; Mike Wesley: 33, 43, 44, 62, 68.

# Table of Contents

Hi, I'm Ginger!

Hi, I'm Sam!

**Let's Start**

**Let's Learn**

**Let's Learn More**

**The Alphabet**

**Let's Build**

**Units Review**

**Let's Learn About**

## Let's Start

### A. Let's talk. CD 1 02

Hi, what's your name?

I'm Kate.

### B. Say and act. CD 1 03

1. What's your name?

_____.

2. _____?

I'm Ginger.

3. What's your name?

# C. Let's sing.

## Hi, What's Your Name?

Hi, what's your name?
　I'm Kate.
Hi, what's your name?
　I'm Jenny.

Hi, what's your name?
　I'm Scott.
Hi, what's your name?
　I'm Andy.

Kate, Jenny, Scott, Andy—
Kate, Jenny, Scott, Andy—
Jenny, Andy, Jenny, Andy—
Kate, Jenny, Scott!

Kate

Jenny

Scott

Andy

# D. Let's move.

1. Stand up.

2. Sit down.

# E. Listen and do.

# Let's Learn

It's a ball.

## A. Words.  CD 1 07

1. a ball

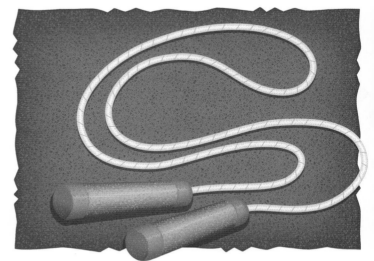

2. a jump rope

3. a yo-yo

4. a bicycle

## B. Listen and point. CD 1 08

# C. Sentences.

It's a yo-yo.

# D. Listen, point, and sing.

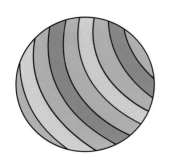 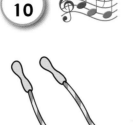 

 What is it? It's a train.

# Let's Learn More

## A. Words.  CD 1 11

1. a train

2. a car

3. a doll

4. a teddy bear

## B. Listen and point.  CD 1 12

# C. Question and answer.

# D. Listen, point, and sing. CD 1 14

# The Alphabet

**A. Sing and say.**

**B. Letters.**

## Let's Build

## A. Ask.  CD 1 17

Hi, what's your name?

1. I'm Pete.

2. I'm Beth.

3. I'm Ann.

4. I'm Matt.

## B. Answer. CD 1 18

What is it?

It's a ball. _____. _____. _____.

# Unit 2 Colors

 Let's Start

## A. Let's talk.  CD 1 19

1.

Hi, boys and girls.

Hello, Miss Jones.

2.

Good-bye.

See you later.

## B. Say and act. CD 1 20

1.

Hi, boys and girls.

_____.

2.

Good-bye.

_____.

## C. Let's sing.

# Hi, Hello, Good-bye

Hi, boys and girls.
  Hello, Miss Jones.
Hi, boys and girls.
  Hello, Miss Jones.
Hi, Andy.
Hello, Jenny.

Good-bye, Kate.
  See you later.
Bye-bye, see you later.
  Bye-bye, see you later.
Bye, Andy,
Good-bye, Jenny.
Good-bye, Kate.
  Bye-bye!

## D. Let's move. CD 1 22

1. Come here.

2. Turn around.

## E. Listen and do. CD 1 23

It's red.

# Let's Learn

## A. Words.

1. red

2. blue

3. yellow

4. green

5. brown

## B. Listen and point.

# C. Sentences.

It's blue.

# D. Listen and point.

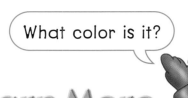
What color is it?

It's purple.

# Let's Learn More

## A. Words.  CD 1 28

1. purple
2. orange
3. black
4. white
5. pink

## B. Listen and point. CD 1 29

# C. Question and answer.

# D. Listen, point, and chant.

# The Alphabet

## A. Sing and say.

ABCDEFGHIJKLMNOPQRSTUVWXYZ

abcdefghijklmnopqrstuvwxyz

## B. Letters and words.

1. **Aa**

apple

2. **Bb**

bird

3. **Cc**

cat

4. **Dd**

dog

## C. Find the letters.

# Let's Build

## A. Sentences. CD 1 34

**It's a red train.**

1. a red train

2. a blue ball

3. a brown teddy bear

4. a green yo-yo

## B. Question and answer. CD 1 35

What is it?

It's a green car.

## A. Listen and circle.  CD 1 36

1.

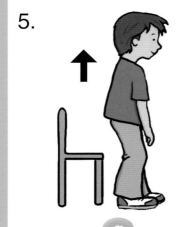

a    b

2.

a    b

3.

a    b

4.

a    b

5.

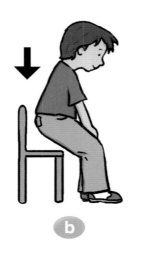

a    b

6.

a    b

# School Supplies

## A. Say these.

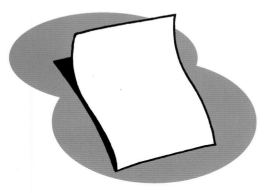

1. paper

2. scissors

3. glue

5. tape

4. paint

I have paper.

# Unit 3 Shapes

## Let's Start

## A. Let's talk. (CD 1 38)

How are you today?

I'm fine, thank you.

## B. Say and act. (CD 1 39)

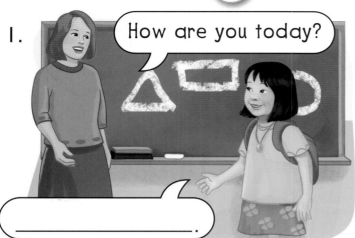

1. How are you today?

_____.

2. _____.

I'm fine, thank you.

## C. Let's sing.

# How Are You Today?

How are you today?
    I'm fine, thank you.
How are you?
    I'm fine, thank you.
How are you today?
    I'm fine, thank you.
How are you?
    I'm fine.

## D. Let's move.

1. Walk.

2. Run.

## E. Listen and do.

## Let's Learn

Draw a circle.

### A. Words.

1. a circle

2. a square

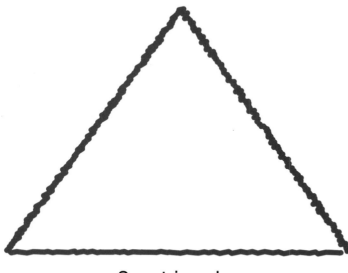

3. a triangle

4. a heart

### B. Listen and point.

# C. Sentences. CD 1 45

# D. Listen, point, and chant. CD 1 46

# Let's Learn More

Is it a star?

Yes, it is.

## A. Words. CD 1 47

1. a star

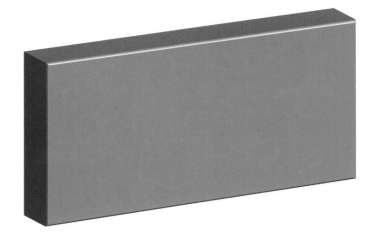

2. a rectangle

3. a diamond

4. an oval

## B. Listen and point. CD 1 48

# C. Question and answer.

# D. Listen, point, and sing.

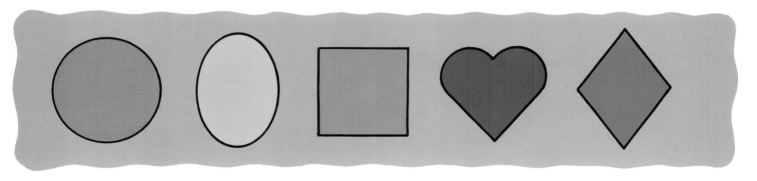

# The Alphabet

## A. Sing and say. CD 1 51

ABCDEFGHIJKLMNOPQRSTUVWXYZ

abcdefghijklmnopqrstuvwxyz

## B. Letters and words. CD 1 52

1. **Ee**

egg

2. **Ff**

fish

3. **Gg**

gorilla

4. **Hh**

heart

## C. Find the letters.

Let's Build

## A. Sentences.  CD 1 53

 It's a blue square.

1. a blue square

2. a purple heart

3. an orange triangle

4. a yellow circle

## B. Question and answer. CD 1 54

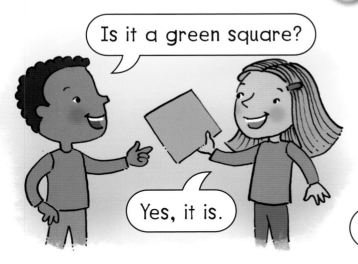

Is it a green square?

Yes, it is.

Is it a red square?

No, it isn't. It's a pink heart.

 1.

 2.

 3.

 4.

 5.

 6.

 7.

 8.

 ## Let's Start

## A. Let's talk. (CD 1 55)

## B. Say and act. (CD 1 56)

1.

2.

## C. Let's sing.

### May I Come In?

May I come in?
   Sure! Please come in!
   Please come in!
May I come in?
May I come in?
   Sure! Please come in!

## D. Let's move.

1. Go.

2. Stop.

## E. Listen and do.

Let's count. 1, 2, 3.

 # Let's Learn

## A. Numbers. (CD 1 60)

1

2

3

4

5

## B. Listen and point. (CD 1 61)

# C. Sentences.

# D. Listen, point, and sing. CD 1 63

How many?

6.

# Let's Learn More

## A. Numbers.
CD 1 64

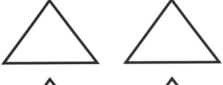

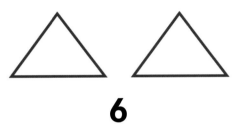

**6**

**8**

**9**

**7**

**10**

## B. Listen and point.
CD 1 65

# C. Question and answer.

# D. Listen, point, and sing.

# The Alphabet

## A. Sing and say.

ABCDEFGHIJKLMNOPQRSTUVWXYZ

abcdefghijklmnopqrstuvwxyz

## B. Letters and words.

1. **Ii** — igloo

2. **Jj** — jump rope

3. **Kk** — kangaroo

4. **Ll** — lion

## C. Find the letters.

# Let's Build

## A. Ask and answer. (CD 1 70)

## B. Find the numbers.

## A. Listen and circle.  (CD 1 71)

1.

ⓐ    ⓑ

2.

ⓐ    ⓑ

3.
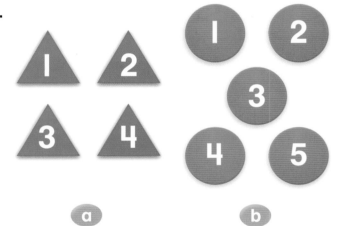
ⓐ    ⓑ

4.
ⓐ    ⓑ

5.

ⓐ    ⓑ

6.

ⓐ    ⓑ

# Classroom Commands

**A. Say these.**

1. Take out your pencil.

2. Put away your pencil.

3. Open your book.

4. Close your book.

Please take out your pencil.

## Let's Start

## A. Let's talk. CD 2 02

Here you are.

Thank you.

DOG FOOD

DOG FOOD

DOG FOOD

3.00

## B. Say and act. CD 2 03

1.

Here you are.

_____.

2.

_____.

Thank you.

## C. Let's sing.

# Here You Are.
# Thank You.

Here you are.
　Thank you, thank you!
Here you are.
　Thank you!
Here you are.
　Thank you, thank you!
Here you are.
　Thank you!

## D. Let's move.

1. Jump.

2. Skip.

## E. Listen and do.

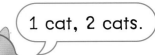

Let's count the cats.

1 cat, 2 cats.

# Let's Learn

## A. Words.  CD 2 07

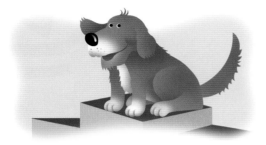

1. dog

2. dogs

3. cat

4. cats

5. bird

6. birds

## B. Listen and point.  CD 2 08

# C. Sentences.

# D. Listen, point, and sing.

How many ducks?

3 ducks.

# Let's Learn More

## A. Words. CD 2 11

cows 2

cow 1

rabbit 3

rabbits 4

duck 5

ducks 6

## B. Listen and point. CD 2 12

## C. Question and answer. CD 2 13

## D. Listen and point. CD 2 14

## E. Listen, point, and sing. CD 2 15

# The Alphabet

## A. Sing and say. CD 2 16

ABCDEFGHIJKLMNOPQRSTUVWXYZ

a b c d e f g h i j k l m n o p q r s t u v w x y z

## B. Letters and words. CD 2 17

1. **Mm**

2. **Nn**

3. **Oo**

4. **Pp**

moon               nest               octopus               peach

## C. Find the letters.

# Let's Build

## A. Count.  CD 2 18

*Let's count.*

*1 train, 2 trains, 3 trains.*

## B. Question and answer. CD 2 19

*How many cars?*

*8 cars.*

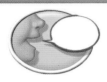 ## Let's Start

## A. Let's talk. CD 2 20

How old are you?

I'm 6.

## B. Say and act. CD 2 21

1.

How old are you?

_____.

2.

_____?

I'm 10.

## C. Let's sing.

### How Old Are You?

How old are you?
I'm 6.
How old are you?
I'm 7.
1, 2, 3, 4, 5, 6, 7!

How old are you?
I'm 5.
How old are you?
I'm 10.
1, 2, 3, 4, 5, 6, 7, 8, 9, 10!

## D. Let's move.

1. Make a line.

2. Make a circle.

## E. Listen and do.

I like ice cream.

## Let's Learn

## A. Words.

1. ice cream

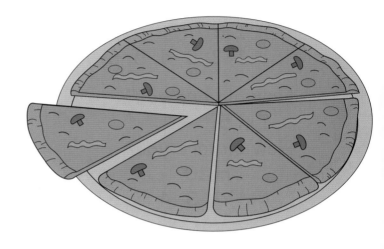

2. pizza

3. cake

4. chicken

## B. Listen and point.

# C. Sentences.

I like cake.

# D. Listen, point, and sing.

Do you like milk?

Yes, I do.

# Let's Learn More

## A. Words.

1. milk

2. fish

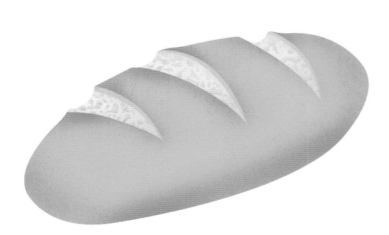

3. bread

4. rice

## B. Listen, point, and chant.

# C. Question and answer.

Do you like fish?

Yes, I do.

No, I don't.

1.

2.

3.

4.

5.

6.

# D. Ask and answer.

 **1**

 **2**

 Do you like milk?

 **3**

 **4**

# The Alphabet

## A. Sing and say.  CD 1 32

ABCDEFGHIJKLMNOPQRSTUVWXYZ

a b c d e f g h i j k l m n o p q r s t u v w x y z

## B. Letters and words.  CD 2 33

1. **Qq**

queen

2. **Rr**

rabbit

3. **Ss**

sun

4. **Tt**

tiger

## C. Find the letters.

# Let's Build

## A. Play a game. CD 1 34

# Units 5-6　Listen and Review

## A. Listen and circle.

1.
　a　　　　　b

2.
　a　　　　　b

3.
　a　　　　　b

4.
　a　　　　　b

5.
　a　　　　　b

6.
　a　　　　　b

# The Weather

## A. Say these. CD 2 36

1. sunny

2. cloudy

3. windy

5. snowy

4. rainy

It's sunny.

# Unit 7 My Body

## Let's Start

**A. Let's talk.** (CD 2 37)

Oops! I'm sorry.

That's OK.

**B. Say and act.** (CD 2 38)

1.

Oops! I'm sorry.

_____.

2.

_____.

That's OK.

# C. Let's sing.

## Oops! I'm Sorry

Oops! I'm sorry.
That's OK.
Oops! I'm sorry,
Oops! I'm sorry.

Oops! I'm sorry.
That's OK.
Oops! I'm sorry.
That's OK.

# D. Let's move.

1. Stamp your feet.

2. Clap your hands.

# E. Listen and do.

# Let's Learn

I can touch my head.

## A. Words. CD 2 42

1. head

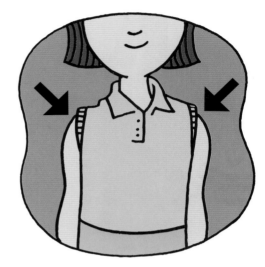

2. shoulders

3. knees

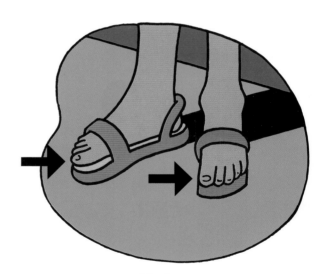

4. toes

## B. Listen and point. CD 2 43

# C. Sentences.

I can touch my head.

# D. Listen, chant, and do.

# Let's Learn More

## A. Words.  CD 2 46

1. eyes

2. ears

3. mouth

4. nose

## B. Listen and point.  CD 2 47

## C. Question and answer.

## D. Listen, sing, and do. CD 2 49

 **The Alphabet**

## A. Sing and say.  CD 2 50

A B C D E F G H I J K L M N O P Q R S T U V W X Y Z
a b c d e f g h i j k l m n o p q r s t u v w x y z

## B. Letters and words. CD 2 51

1. **Uu**

umbrella

2. **Vv**

violin

3. **Ww**

watch

## C. Find the letters.

# Let's Build

## A. Sentences.  CD 2 52

I can touch the red circle.

## B. Question and answer. CD 2 53

What can you do?

I can touch the red circle.

## Let's Start

## A. Let's talk. (CD 2 54)

Let's play.

OK. Let's play ball.

OK. Let's play tag.

OK. Let's jump rope.

## B. Say and act. (CD 2 55)

1.

Let's play.

_____.

2.

_____.

OK. Let's jump rope.

## C. Let's sing.  CD 2 56

**Let's Play**

Let's play.
  OK!
Let's play.
  OK, OK!
Let's play, let's play.
  OK, let's play!

Let's play tag.
  OK, let's play, let's play!
Let's jump rope.
  OK, OK, let's play!
Let's play ball.
  OK, let's play, let's play!
Hey, let's play, let's play!
  OK!

## D. Let's move. CD 2 57

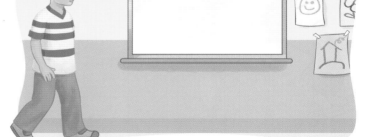

1. Point to the board.          2. Go to the board.

## E. Listen and do. CD 2 58

## Let's Learn

I can ride a bicycle.

**A. Words.**  CD 2 59

1. ride a bicycle

2. sing a song

3. fly a kite

4. bounce a ball

**B. Listen and point.**  CD 2 60

# C. Sentences. CD 2 61

# D. Listen, point, and chant. CD 2 62

Can you swim?

No, I can't.

# Let's Learn More

## A. Words.

1. swim

2. smile

3. wink

4. dance

## B. Listen and point.

# C. Question and answer.

**Can you dance?**

**Yes, I can.**

**Can you dance?**

**No, I can't.**

# D. Listen and chant.

# The Alphabet

## A. Sing and say.  CD 2 67

$$\boxed{\begin{array}{l} \text{A B C D E F G H I J K L M N O P Q R S T U V W X Y Z} \\ \text{a b c d e f g h i j k l m n o p q r s t u v w x y z} \end{array}}$$

## B. Letters and words. CD 2 68

1. **Xx**

fox

2. **Yy**

yarn

3. **Zz**

zebra

## C. Find the letters.

# Let's Build

## A. Play a game.

# Units 7-8  Listen and Review

## A. Listen and circle. CD 2 70

1.
   (a)      (b)

2.
   (a)      (b)

3.
   (a)      (b)

4.
   (a)      (b)

5.
   (a)      (b)

6.
   (a)      (b)

# Days of the Week

## A. Say these. CD 2 71

Sunday 1

Monday 2

Tuesday 3

Wednesday 4

Thursday 5

Friday 6

Saturday 7

It's Monday.

## B. Let's sing. CD 2 72

# Let's Begin Syllabus

## Unit 1    Toys

| Let's Start | Let's Learn | Let's Learn More | The Alphabet | Let's Build |
|---|---|---|---|---|
| Hi! What's your name? I'm Kate. Asking someone's name<br><br>Stand up. Commands | ball<br><br>It's a ball. Identifying objects (singular) | train<br><br>What is it? It's a train. Asking about objects | Alphabet song Aa-Zz Learning the Alphabet | What's your name? I'm Pete. Learning new names |

## Unit 2    Colors

| Let's Start | Let's Learn | Let's Learn More | The Alphabet | Let's Build |
|---|---|---|---|---|
| Hi, boys and girls. Hello, Miss Jones. Good-bye. See you later. Saying hello and good-bye | red<br><br>It's red. Identifying colors | purple<br><br>What color is it? It's purple. Asking about and identifying colors | Alphabet song Aa-Zz<br><br>Alphabet A-D apple bird cat dog Practicing the Alphabet | It's a red train.<br><br>What is it? It's a red train.<br><br>Using colors as adjectives |

| Units 1–2 Listen and Review | School Supplies I have paper. |
|---|---|

## Unit 3    Shapes

| Let's Start | Let's Learn | Let's Learn More | The Alphabet | Let's Build |
|---|---|---|---|---|
| How are you today? I'm fine, thank you. Greetings<br><br>Walk. Commands | circle<br><br>Draw a circle. Introducing shapes and having students draw them | star<br><br>Is it a star? Yes, it is. Identifying more shapes | Alphabet song Aa-Zz<br><br>Alphabet E-H egg fish gorilla heart Practicing the Alphabet | It's a blue square.<br><br>Is it a green square? Yes, it is. No, it isn't. It's a pink heart. Asking and answering about colored shapes |

# Unit 4　Numbers

| Let's Start | Let's Learn | Let's Learn More | The Alphabet | Let's Build |
|---|---|---|---|---|
| May I come in? Sure! Please come in! Asking permission to enter a place<br><br>Go. Commands | Let's count. 1, 2, 3… Identifying numbers and counting objects (1-5) | How many? 6. Identifying numbers and counting objects (6-10) | Alphabet song Aa-Zz<br><br>Alphabet I-L igloo jump rope kangaroo lion Practicing the Alphabet | Is it a 9? Yes, it is. No, it isn't. It's a 6. Identifying numbers |

**Units 3–4 Listen and Review**　　　**Classroom Commands**
Please take out your pencil.

# Unit 5　Animals

| Let's Start | Let's Learn | Let's Learn More | The Alphabet | Let's Build |
|---|---|---|---|---|
| Here you are. Thank you. Giving and receiving<br><br>Jump. Commands | cat, cats<br><br>Let's count the cats. 1 cat, 2 cats. Counting, identifying singular and plural items | duck, ducks<br><br>How many ducks? 3 ducks. Counting, identifying singular and plural items | Alphabet song Aa-Zz<br><br>Alphabet M-P moon nest octopus peach Practicing the Alphabet | Let's count. 1 train, 2 trains, 3 trains.<br><br>How many cars? 8 cars. Counting, identifying singular and plural items |

# Unit 6　Food

| Let's Start | Let's Learn | Let's Learn More | The Alphabet | Let's Build |
|---|---|---|---|---|
| How old are you? I'm 6. Asking and telling someone's age<br><br>Make a line. Commands | ice cream<br><br>I like ice cream. Expressing likes about food | milk<br><br>Do you like milk? Yes, I do. No, I don't. Expressing likes and dislikes about food | Alphabet song Aa-Zz<br><br>Alphabet Q-T queen rabbit sun tiger Practicing the Alphabet | Do you like birds? Yes, I do. No, I don't. Asking about likes and dislikes |

# Let's Begin Syllabus

| Units 5–6 Listen and Review | The Weather |
| --- | --- |
| | It's sunny. |

## Unit 7 My Body

| Let's Start | Let's Learn | Let's Learn More | The Alphabet | Let's Build |
| --- | --- | --- | --- | --- |
| Oops! I'm sorry! That's OK. Apologizing | head | nose | Alphabet song Aa-Zz | I can touch the red circle. |
| | I can touch my head. Expressing ability | What can you do? I can touch my nose. Asking about ability | Alphabet U-W umbrella violin watch Practicing the Alphabet | What can you do? I can touch the red circle. Asking and answering about ability |
| Stamp your feet. Commands | | | | |

## Unit 8 Abilities

| Let's Start | Let's Learn | Let's Learn More | The Alphabet | Let's Build |
| --- | --- | --- | --- | --- |
| Let's play. OK. Let's play ball. Inviting friends to play | ride a bicycle | swim | Alphabet song Aa-Zz | Can you jump? Yes, I can. Asking and answering about ability |
| | I can/can't ride a bicycle. Expressing ability and inability | Can you swim? Yes, I can. No, I can't. Expressing ability and inability | Alphabet X-Z fox yarn zebra Practicing the Alphabet | |
| Point to the board. Commands | | | | |

| Units 7–8 Listen and Review | Days of the Week |
| --- | --- |
| | It's Monday. Learning the days of the week |

# Teacher and Student Card List Let's Begin

| | | | | | | | |
|---|---|---|---|---|---|---|---|
| 1 | Stand up. | 51 | 4 | 101 | rainy |
| 2 | Sit down. | 52 | 5 | 102 | snowy |
| 3 | a ball | 53 | 6 | 103 | Stamp your feet. |
| 4 | a jump rope | 54 | 7 | 104 | Clap your hands. |
| 5 | a yo-yo | 55 | 8 | 105 | head |
| 6 | a bicycle | 56 | 9 | 106 | shoulders |
| 7 | a train | 57 | 10 | 107 | knees |
| 8 | a car | 58 | igloo | 108 | toes |
| 9 | a doll | 59 | jump rope | 109 | eyes |
| 10 | a teddy bear | 60 | kangaroo | 110 | ears |
| 11 | Come here. | 61 | lion | 111 | mouth |
| 12 | Turn around. | 62 | Take out your pencil. | 112 | nose |
| 13 | red | 63 | Put away your pencil. | 113 | umbrella |
| 14 | blue | 64 | Open your book. | 114 | violin |
| 15 | yellow | 65 | Close your book. | 115 | watch |
| 16 | green | 66 | Jump. | 116 | Point to the board. |
| 17 | brown | 67 | Skip. | 117 | Go to the board. |
| 18 | purple | 68 | dog | 118 | ride a bicycle |
| 19 | orange | 69 | dogs | 119 | sing a song |
| 20 | black | 70 | cat | 120 | fly a kite |
| 21 | white | 71 | cats | 121 | bounce a ball |
| 22 | pink | 72 | bird | 122 | swim |
| 23 | apple | 73 | birds | 123 | smile |
| 24 | bird | 74 | cow | 124 | wink |
| 25 | cat | 75 | cows | 125 | dance |
| 26 | dog | 76 | rabbit | 126 | fox |
| 27 | paper | 77 | rabbits | 127 | yarn |
| 28 | scissors | 78 | duck | 128 | zebra |
| 29 | glue | 79 | ducks | 129 | Sunday |
| 30 | paint | 80 | moon | 130 | Monday |
| 31 | tape | 81 | nest | 131 | Tuesday |
| 32 | Walk. | 82 | octopus | 132 | Wednesday |
| 33 | Run. | 83 | peach | 133 | Thursday |
| 34 | a circle | 84 | Make a line. | 134 | Friday |
| 35 | a square | 85 | Make a circle. | 135 | Saturday |
| 36 | a triangle | 86 | ice cream | | |
| 37 | a heart | 87 | pizza | | |
| 38 | a star | 88 | cake | | |
| 39 | a rectangle | 89 | chicken | | |
| 40 | a diamond | 90 | milk | | |
| 41 | an oval | 91 | fish | | |
| 42 | egg | 92 | bread | | |
| 43 | fish | 93 | rice | | |
| 44 | gorilla | 94 | queen | | |
| 45 | heart | 95 | rabbit | | |
| 46 | Go. | 96 | sun | | |
| 47 | Stop. | 97 | tiger | | |
| 48 | 1 | 98 | sunny | | |
| 49 | 2 | 99 | cloudy | | |
| 50 | 3 | 100 | windy | | |

# Word List

**A**

a 4
and 10
apple 16
are 20

**B**

ball 4
bicycle 4
bird 16
birds 40
black 14
blue 12
board 65
book 37
bounce 66
boys 10
bread 50
brown 12

**C**

cake 48
can 58
can't 68
car 6
cars 45
cat 16
cats 40
chicken 48
circle 22
clap 57
close 37
cloudy 55
color 14
come here 11
come in 28
count 30
cow 42
cows 42

**D**

desk 4
dance 68
diamond 24
do 50
dog 16
dogs 40
doll 6

don't 51
draw 23
duck 42
ducks 42

**E**

ears 60
egg 26
eight (8) 32
eyes 60

**F**

feet 57
fine 20
fish 26
five (5) 31
fly 66
four (4) 31
fox 70
Friday 73

**G**

girls 10
glue 19
go 29
good-bye 10
gorilla 26
green 12

**H**

hands 57
have 19
head 58
heart 22
hello 10
here 38
hi 2
how 20
how many 32
how old 46

**I**

ice cream 48
igloo 34
I'm 2
I'm sorry 56
is 6
isn't 25

it 6
it's 4

**J**

jump 39
jump rope 4

**K**

kangaroo 34
kite 66
knees 58

**L**

let's 30
like 48
line 47
lion 34

**M**

make 47
may 28
milk 50
miss 10
Monday 73
moon 44
mouth 60
my 58

**N**

name 2
nest 44
nine (9) 32
no 25
nose 60

**O**

octopus 44
one (1) 30
oops 56
open 37
orange 14
oval 24

**P**

paint 19
paper 19

peach 44
pencil 37
pink 14
pizza 48
play 64
please 28
point 65
purple 14

**Q**

queen 52

**R**

rabbit 42
rabbits 42
rainy 55
rectangle 24
red 12
rice 50
ride 66
run 21

**S**

Saturday 73
scissors 19
see you later 10
seven (7) 32
shoulders 58
sing 66
sit down 3
six (6) 32
skip 39
smile 68
snowy 55
song 66
square 22
stamp 57
stand up 3
star 24
stop 29
sun 52
Sunday 73
sunny 55
sure 28
swim 68

**T**

tag 64

take out 37
tape 19
teddy bear 6
ten (10) 32
thank you 20
that's OK 56
the 65
three (3) 30
Thursday 73
tiger 52
to 65
today 20
toes 58
touch 58
train 6
trains 45
triangle 22
Tuesday 73
turn around 11
two (2) 30

**U**

umbrella 62

**V**

violin 62

**W**

walk 21
watch 62
Wednesday 73
what 6
what's 2
white 14
windy 55
wink 68

**Y**

yarn 70
yellow 12
yes 24
yo-yo 4
you 20
your 2

**Z**

zebra 70